Small Business Goal and Action Planner

- Business Plan Organizer
- Market Research
- Competitive Analysis
- Quarterly Action Planning
- Quarterly and Yearly Review
- Much More!

Exousia House Publishing™

Small Business Goal and Action Planner

Exousia House Publishing™
An Imprint of Exousia House, LLC

320 W. Lanier Avenue, Suite 200
Fayetteville, GA 30214
Phone: (404) 997-3502
www.ExousiaHouse.com

Printed in the United States of America

ISBN-13: 978-0-9768631-2-0

Designed by: Cynthia W. Moore

THIS PLANNER BELONGS TO:

Part One:

Business Plan Notebook

Business Plan Checklist

Executive Summary

- [ ] Name, Location, and Contact Information
- [ ] Strategic Direction
- [ ] Purpose of Plan

Company Summary

- [ ] Business Structure
- [ ] Mission and Vision Statements
- [ ] Products and Services

Market Analysis

- [ ] Industry Research
- [ ] Target Market
- [ ] Competitive Analysis
- [ ] Competitive Edge
- [ ] Customer Persona
- [ ] Marketing Strategy
- [ ] Pricing
- [ ] Distribution
- [ ] Sales Forecasts

Financial Summary

- [ ] Startup Costs or Current Financial Position
- [ ] Profit and Loss Statement
- [ ] Cash Flow Statement
- [ ] Balance Sheet
- [ ] Break-Even Analysis
- [ ] Financial Projections

Management Summary

- [ ] Management Team
- [ ] Partnerships and Advisors
- [ ] Ownership and Contingency Plan

Conclusion

- [ ] Summarize Opportunities and Vision

NOTES :

EXECUTIVE SUMMARY

STRATEGIC DIRECTION - PURPOSE

COMPANY SUMMARY

VISION

MISSION

PRODUCTS AND SERVICES

MARKET RESEARCH - INDUSTRY

MARKET TRENDS

TARGET MARKET

COMPETITIVE ANALYSIS

COMPETITIVE EDGE

CUSTOMER PERSONA

CUSTOMER EXPERIENCE

MARKETING STRATEGY-PROMOTION

MARKETING STRATEGY-ADS

WEBSITE PLANNER

WEBSITE PLANNER

PRICING

DISTRIBUTION

SALES FORECAST

STARTUP OR CURRENT FINANCES

FINANCIAL - PROFIT & LOSS

FINANCIAL - CASH FLOW

FINANCIAL - BALANCE SHEET

FINANCIAL BREAK-EVEN ANALYSIS

FUNDING SOURCES

FINANCIAL - PROJECTIONS

MANAGEMENT TEAM

PARTNERSHIPS AND ADVISORS

OWNERSHIP - CONTINGENCY PLAN

CONCLUSION

Part Two:

Goal and Action Planner

YEARLY GOALS

YEARLY GOALS

YEAR AT-A-GLANCE

January

February

March

April

May

June

YEAR AT-A-GLANCE

July	
August	
September	
October	
November	
December	

QUARTERLY GOALS FOR

QUARTERLY GOALS FOR

ACTION PLAN FOR

TO-DO

ACTION PLAN FOR

TO-DO

ACTION PLAN FOR

TO-DO

ACTION PLAN FOR

TO-DO

ACTION PLAN FOR

TO-DO

QUARTERLY REVIEW FOR

QUARTERLY REVIEW FOR

QUARTERLY GOALS FOR

QUARTERLY GOALS FOR

ACTION PLAN FOR

TO-DO

ACTION PLAN FOR

TO-DO

ACTION PLAN FOR

TO-DO

ACTION PLAN FOR

TO-DO

ACTION PLAN FOR

TO-DO

QUARTERLY REVIEW FOR

QUARTERLY REVIEW FOR

QUARTERLY GOALS FOR

QUARTERLY GOALS FOR

ACTION PLAN FOR

TO-DO

ACTION PLAN FOR

TO-DO

ACTION PLAN FOR

TO-DO

ACTION PLAN FOR

TO-DO

ACTION PLAN FOR

TO-DO

QUARTERLY REVIEW FOR

QUARTERLY REVIEW FOR

QUARTERLY GOALS FOR

QUARTERLY GOALS FOR

ACTION PLAN FOR

TO-DO

ACTION PLAN FOR

TO-DO

ACTION PLAN FOR

TO-DO

ACTION PLAN FOR

TO-DO

ACTION PLAN FOR

TO-DO

QUARTERLY REVIEW FOR

QUARTERLY REVIEW FOR

YEARLY REVIEW - HIGHLIGHTS

YEARLY REVIEW - SUCCESSES

YEARLY REVIEW - NEEDS IMPROVING

NOTES

NOTES

NOTES

NOTES

NOTES

Made in the USA
Monee, IL
08 November 2026

67971464R00063